The Science of Warfare

The Ferocious Facts About How We Fight

written by
Roger Canavan

BOOK HOUSE
a SALARIYA *imprint*

Contents

Author:
Roger Canavan is an award-winning author of more than 60 books for young readers, covering science and other non-fiction subjects. Regular school visits and science experiments conducted with his three children keep him connected with his wide readership as well as with the latest school curriculum developments.

Series creator:
David Salariya was born in Dundee, Scotland. He has illustrated a wide range of books and has created and designed many new series for publishers in the UK and overseas. David established The Salariya Book Company in 1989. He lives in Brighton with his wife, illustrator Shirley Willis, and their son Jonathan.

Artists: Sadie McEwan, Bryan Beach, Jared Green, Sam Bridges and Shutterstock.

Editor:
Nick Pierce

Published in Great Britain in MMXIX by Book House, an imprint of
The Salariya Book Company Ltd
25 Marlborough Place, Brighton BN1 1UB
www.salariya.com

PB ISBN: 978-1-912537-65-5

SALARIYA
SCRIBO   BOOK HOUSE   SCRIBBLERS

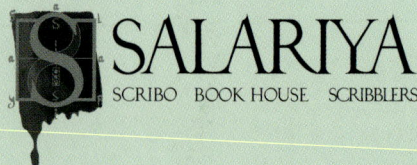

1 3 5 7 9 8 6 4 2

A CIP catalogue record for this book is available from the British Library.

Printed and bound in China.

Visit
www.salariya.com
for our online catalogue and **free** fun stuff.

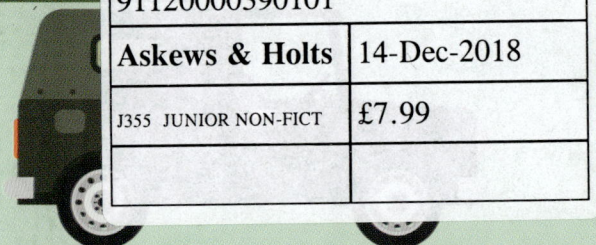

PAPER FROM
SUSTAINABLE
FORESTS

Introduction

Whether it's disagreements about football teams, arguments about who won an election or conflict over which country really owns some valuable gold mines, human beings often seem to be in conflict. The most serious and wide-ranging disagreements can develop into deadly battles and wars.

Another natural human quality is curiosity. It drives our quest for knowledge and easier ways to do things. And it's through science and its relative, technology (which finds practical uses for scientific advances), that we can observe human progress. Can you imagine a time without television, or cars... or even the wheel? You can thank science and scientists for much of the world around you.

So it's not surprising that throughout history, people have turned to science to give themselves an advantage in their conflicts. In the following pages you'll have a chance to see how science is the driving force that lets rifles fire straight, massive battleships stay afloat and lasers pinpoint their targets from high above the ground.

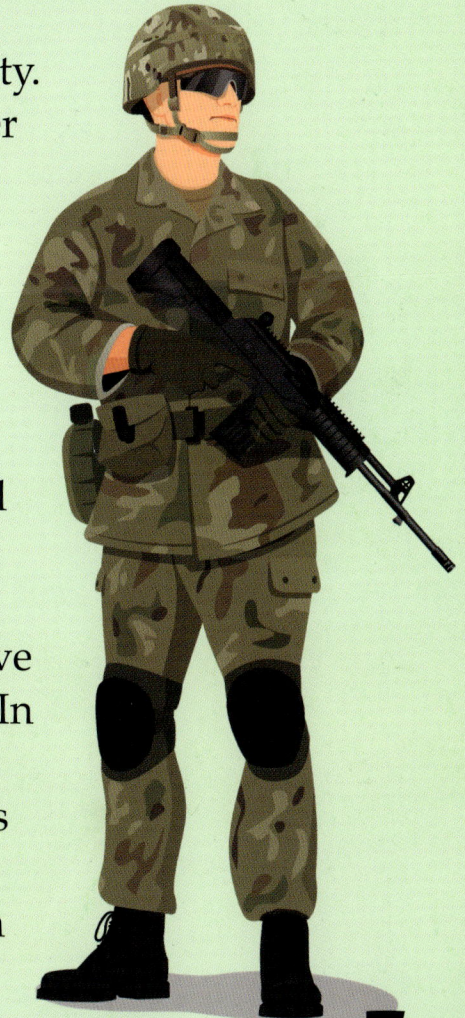

Judo and other martial arts use no weapons, but players can judge an opponent's centre of mass (their balancing point) and up-end him or her more easily.

Some animals can use sticks, stones, or sometimes simply the force of gravity to get food. But the big difference between even the cleverest animals and ourselves is the way that humans can not only come up with ideas, but improve on them quickly. And it's an awareness – even unconsciously – of science that gives humans the edge.

Even the earliest humans harnessed technology, the practical application of science, to create tools and weapons. Always observing the effect of different forces, those primitive peoples laid the foundation for later advances.

Hand to hand combat

The earliest form of fighting – with no weapons apart from the body itself – can still be seen in the modern world, mainly in wrestling, boxing and the martial arts.

Spears

Humans first carved tips of wooden poles to create spears at least 400,000 years ago. Later spears had tips made of sharpened stones attached to the pole. Spears can be thrown to attack prey or enemies, but they can also be used in close combat.

The spear-thrower would instinctively use scientific techniques to design the best spear (for balance, distance and accuracy). Defending against these weapons also called for science: shields and armour needed to be strong enough to withstand the force of a moving spear.

Bow and arrow

The bow and arrow is an excellent example of potential energy building up (as the bow is pulled) and then turned into kinetic (movement) energy as it's released.

The English victory over the French at Agincourt in 1415 was largely thanks to the scientific advantage (extra force) provided by their new weapon: the longbow.

Can you believe it?

Spear-throwers, like the atlatls used by Aztec warriors, utilised basic science. A throwing arm acts like a lever and the spear-thrower handle lengthens that lever, providing more force.

Atlatl

The crossbow used the same principle as the bow and arrow but released far more kinetic energy – so that the bolt fired (like a mini-arrow) could pierce metal armour.

The arms race

People are natural scientists – constantly testing objects and activities for the best results – and this scientific curiosity led to constant development of weapons. Over the centuries these weapons became sharper and more explosive.

Defensive fortresses such as castles had to cope with the pummelling of siege engines, such as trebuchets, and eventually the destructive force of gunpowder, which was developed in China, but spread across Asia and Europe.

Damascus steel

Swords from the Middle East during the Medieval era had a particular advantage: the best were made from Damascus steel, making blades tough, resistant to shattering and easy to sharpen to an extreme edge. The scientific and technical explanation? It's a mystery, since the technique was abandoned in the eighteenth century.

Gunpowder

Gunpowder was invented in China as early as the year 142 AD. By the tenth century, Chinese armies were harnessing its explosive power to create fire arrows that could be launched at enemies. The burning gunpowder had become rocket fuel.

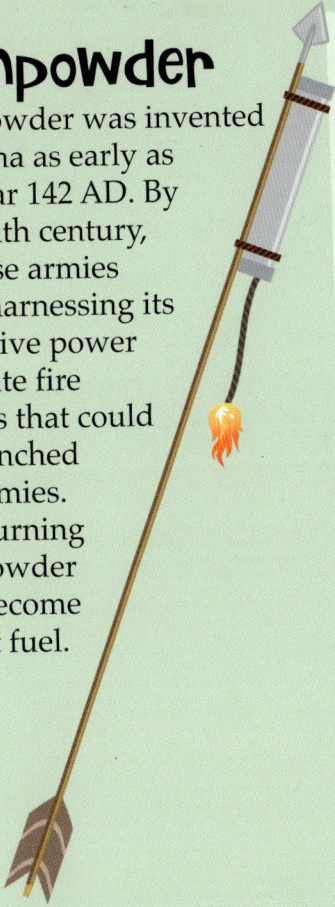

Siege mentality

A trebuchet was a medieval weapon that used a long arm on a hinge to hurl heavy objects long distances. The long arm would be cranked downward, lifting a counterweight (on the other arm) upward. When the counterweight was released, the force of gravity was transferred into kinetic energy so that the long arm swung forward and hurled its payload.

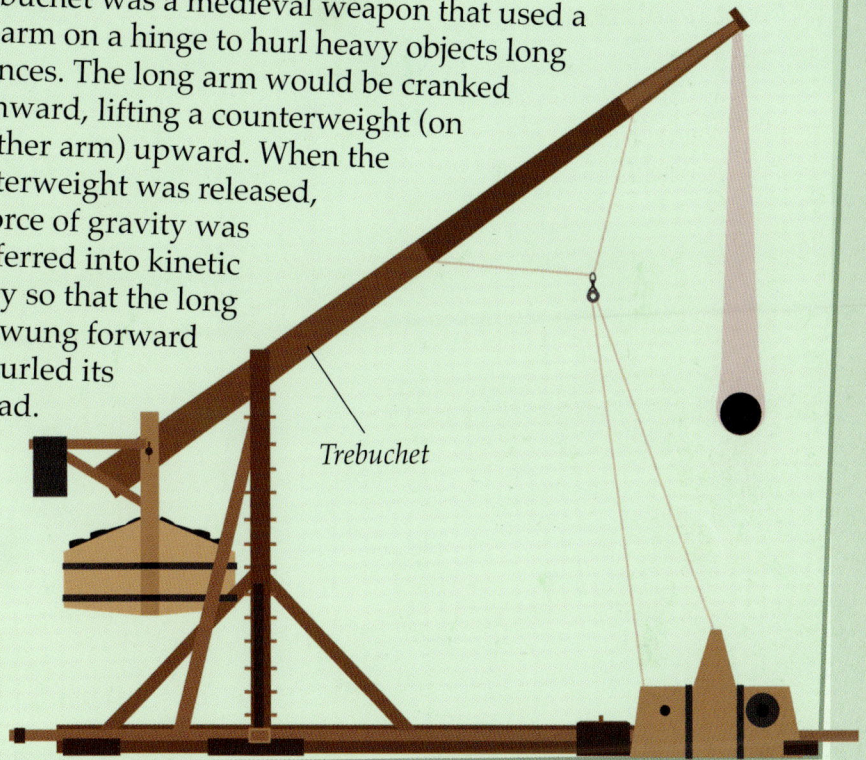

Trebuchet

Try it yourself

You can build a simple siege weapon easily. Glue a plastic egg cup to the end of a ruler and rest the ruler on a pencil so that it's like a see-saw. Load a grape into the egg cup then strike the other end of the ruler to launch the grape.

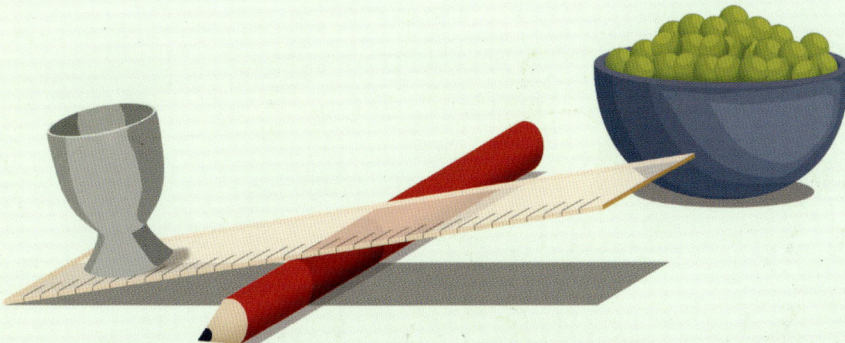

Science has been used in defence from the earliest times. Iron Age forts in Britain occupied hills, with defensive ditches surrounding them. The ditches were placed far enough apart so that the stones flung by attackers would fall short.

The guns of war

Early firearms were unreliable and the force of the explosion would sometimes injure the soldier rather than direct the shot outwards.

Knowledge of the explosive power of gunpowder spread from Asia to Europe in the Middle Ages. Earlier weapons – such as spears, bows and arrows, and lances – gradually became obsolete. Science had ushered in an age of much more powerful weapons.

Technology enabled armed forces to make these new weapons more accurate, so that explosive shells could reach targets many kilometres (miles) away. And modern hand-held weapons allow soldiers to fire more than 1,000 rounds per minute.

Muskets

By the eighteenth century, soldiers fired muskets by pulling a trigger. This would cause a flint-tipped hammer to strike metal and create a spark, making the gunpowder ignite.

Rifles

Angular momentum is the measure of how a spinning object remains stable. One example is a bicycle becoming more stable as its wheels spin faster. Another would be a spinning rifle bullet remaining stable ('on target') once it's fired.

Automatic weapons hold ammunition in a case attached to the gun, allowing a soldier to fire a series of shots without reloading.

Cannons

Large-scale artillery combined the basic scientific principles of gunpowder and other explosives to send shells long distances. During the Second World War, British and German cannons duelled across the English Channel. Two of the largest British cannons were nicknamed 'Winnie' and 'Pooh'.

How it works

A series of spiral grooves (called 'rifling') inside the barrel of a rifle causes a bullet to spin as it leaves the weapon. The bullet acquires angular momentum – and greater accuracy – as a result.

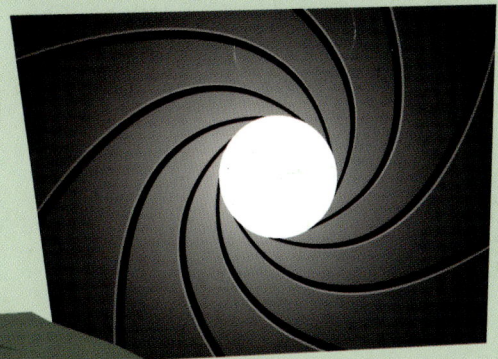

Railways

Both sides in the First World War (1914–18) called on railways to transport troops and equipment. Each division (12,000 soldiers) needed two daily supply trains, each transporting more than 900,000 kilograms of supplies.

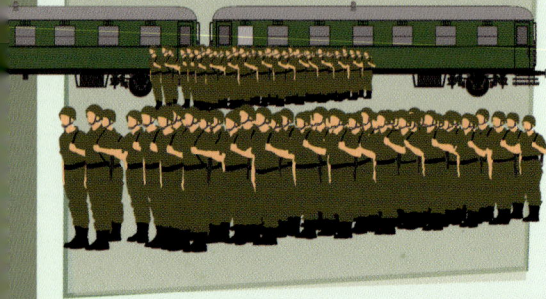

Ready to roll

For centuries armies moved on foot, with animals such as horses and oxen sometimes transporting goods and weapons. But it was slow progress. By the late nineteenth century, advances in transport (especially with trains and powered vehicles) increased mobility considerably.

Many of the new vehicles became effective weapons themselves – and some modern vehicles can detect mines and other dangers. Sophisticated radar and computer equipment means that ground-based vehicles can detect and shoot down airborne missiles and aircraft.

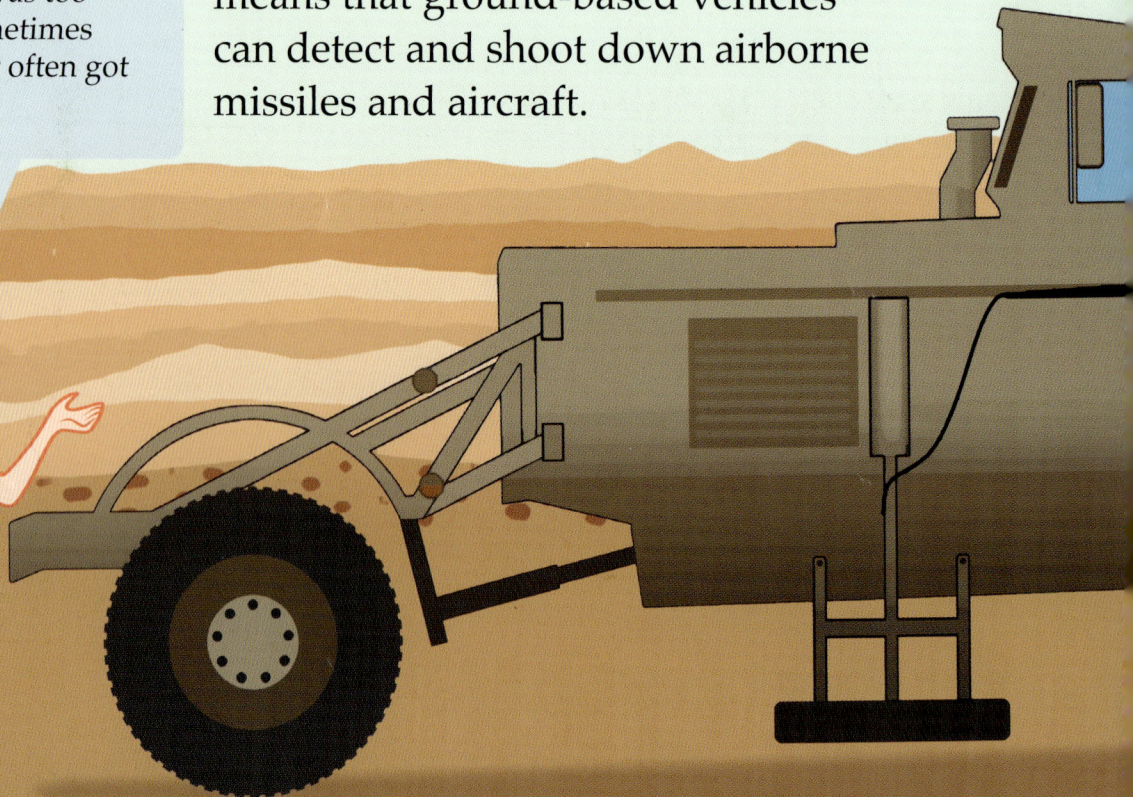

The US Army had real problems with the Sherman tank in the Second World War. Its armour was too thin, its guns sometimes backfired... and it often got stuck in mud.

Tanks

Tanks, which were like mobile fortresses, entered combat in the First World War but became widespread in the Second World War.

Their designs had to combine speed, the ability to navigate difficult terrain and protection against oncoming enemy fire.

Half-track vehicles are designed to have the speed and flexibility of trucks with the traction (grip) of tanks on loose or wet surfaces.

Jeep

A basic technical development (using four- rather than two-wheel drive) created the Jeep, which the famous American General George C. Marshall described as 'America's greatest contribution to modern warfare.'

How it works

The wide tread of tank tracks spreads the enormous mass of the tank across a wide area, so that the tank won't sink as it crosses soft surfaces.

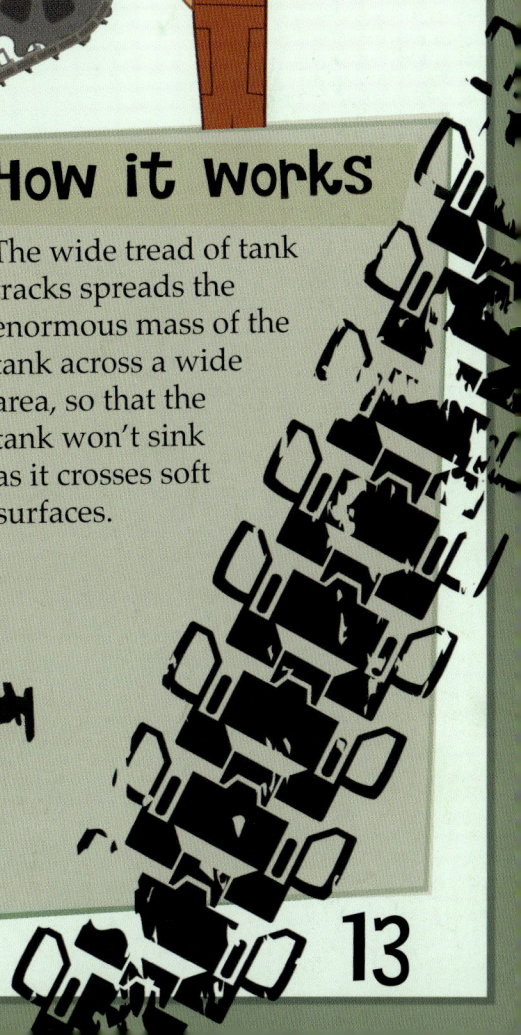

Spanish Armada

Spain's large, bulky vessels in their 1588 naval attack were outmanoeuvred by smaller English ships, which harnessed shifting winds more effectively.

The high seas

Buoyancy, the scientific force that allows even very heavy objects to float, plays a huge role in naval conflicts. People have harnessed that force from earliest prehistory with log rafts and dugout canoes. But today's naval vessels, including massive battleships and aircraft carriers, are using the same fundamental force to sail the high seas.

Cutting-edge technology has also allowed warships (or more precisely, submarines) to cruise underwater for up to 90 days – limited only by the need to top up food supplies.

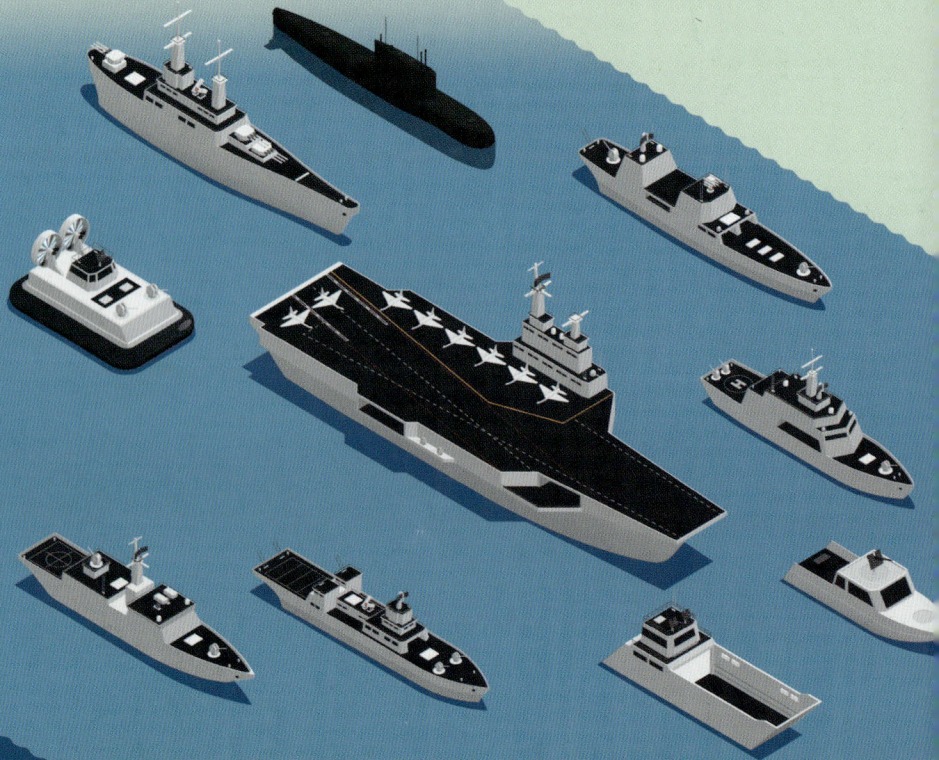

Some nineteenth-century sailing ships could reach speeds of 40 kph (25 mph), matching the speed of powered vessels of the time. But if the wind died, or changed direction, those ships could slow to a standstill.

Submarines

Modern submarines have nuclear fuel, which reacts in a process called fission to produce heat. The heat turns water to steam, driving turbines to produce electricity.

Mobile airfields

An aircraft carrier is designed to provide a mobile landing strip for a fleet of aircraft. The Battle of Midway in 1942 saw Japanese and American aircraft carriers send planes to battle over the Pacific Ocean, far away from the nearest land.

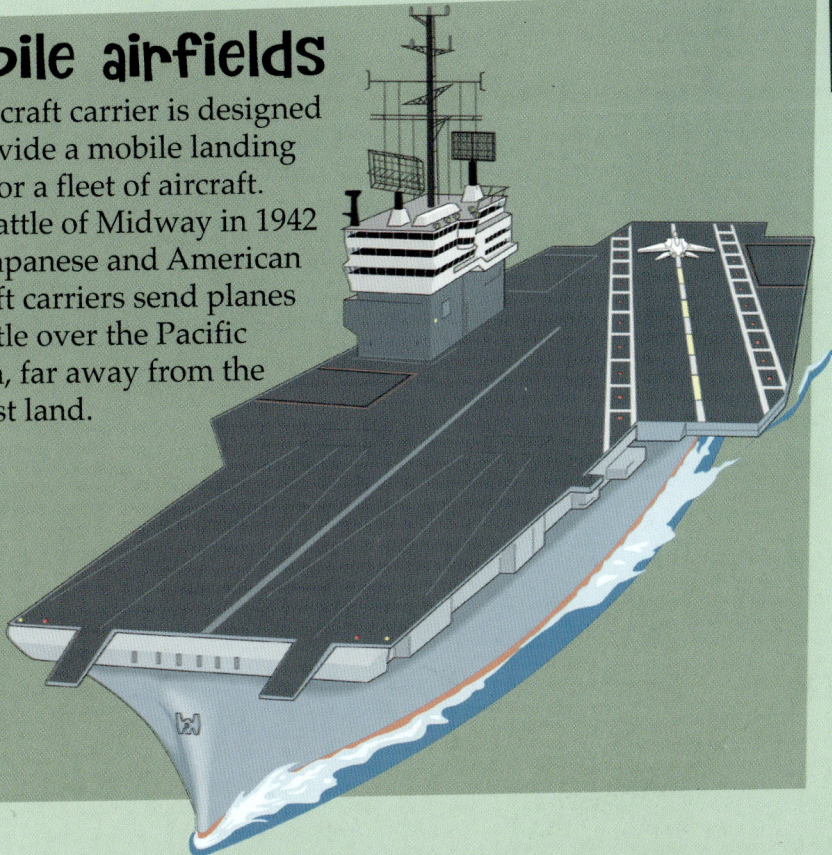

British doctors used vitamin C to prevent the wasting disease scurvy, which affected sailors on long voyages in the nineteenth century. Eating vitamin-rich limes helped British sailors remain healthy.

The machine guns on First World War fighters fired directly through the path of the plane's propeller. The gun's firing rhythm had to match that of the propeller so that the bullets would pass between the spinning propeller blades.

First fighter planes

Each set of wings provides more lift for a plane. Some First World War fighter planes had three sets of wings.

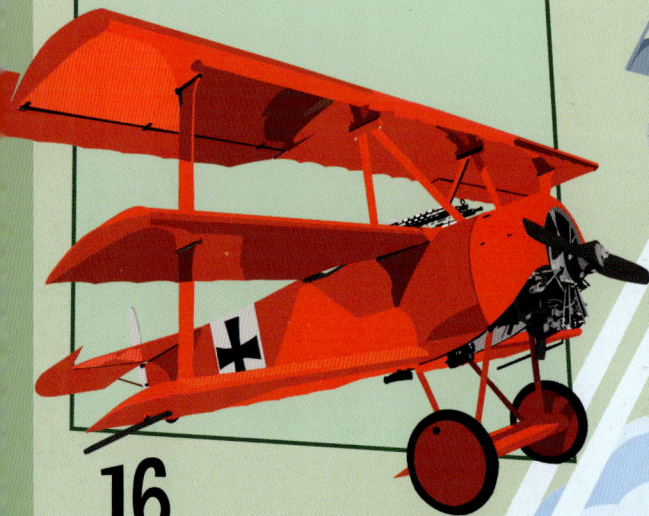

Into the air

Just over a decade after America's Wright brothers developed the first successful powered aircraft, planes were in the air – fighting each other and attacking those on the ground.

Three forces are at work as an aircraft flies. Its forward motion generates lift (an upward force). This must be greater than the drag – the 'air resistance' force as the aircraft moves forward – and the force of gravity. Overcoming lift and drag to become airborne was just a first step: military aircraft soon harnessed ballistics and explosive force to equip themselves with weapons and powerful bombs.

Sound barrier

Some people worried that any plane 'breaking the sound barrier' (travelling faster than the speed of sound) would be crushed in the process. New jet engines in the 1940s gave planes more speed, and the sound barrier was finally broken – safely – in 1947.

V-2 rockets

In the closing year of the Second World War, German scientists led by Wernher von Braun developed liquid-fuel rockets to attack Great Britain and other countries in Western Europe. The V2s are considered to be the first guided ballistic missiles.

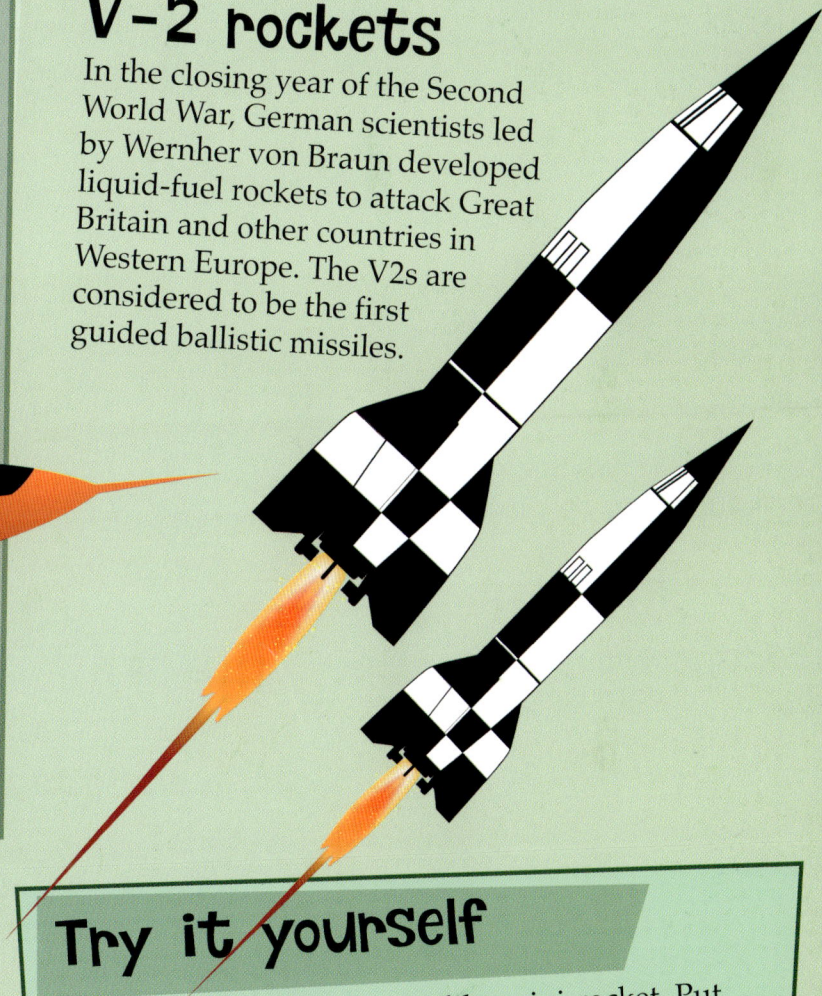

German aerospace engineer Wernher von Braun surrendered to the Americans in 1945 and was recruited to head the US rocket-building programme that eventually sent a man to the Moon.

Try it yourself

Ask an adult to help you build a mini-rocket. Put a quarter teaspoon of baking soda in a small piece of tissue. Twist the tissue closed and tape it to the inside of an old film canister lid. Half fill the canister with vinegar, then clip the cap back on. Turn the canister upside-down and stand by for blast off!

Baking soda

Vinegar

Toilet paper

Film canister

Big Bertha

In the early twentieth century, weapons technicians began building mobile cannons capable of firing enormous loads. Until then, it was felt that cannons with barrels wider than 20 centimetres (8 inches) had to be stationary. Germany's 'Big Bertha', for example, was a mobile cannon that could fire shells weighing 820 kilograms (1,807 pounds).

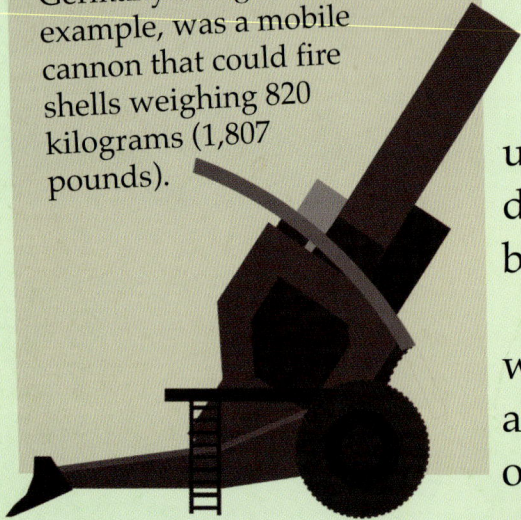

Bombs and shells

The science of explosives is very old, but is constantly being updated, refined and applied to new weapons. Explosives known as shells can be fired from cannons while others can be dropped from aircraft or hidden underground. And then there are weapons that destroy living things, but have no effect on buildings, bridges and other non-living objects.

Despite their differences, all of these explosive weapons depend on some basic science. They all involve a sudden – and destructive – release of energy.

Alfred Nobel, the Swedish scientist who developed dynamite, never wanted his invention to be used in warfare. He set up the Nobel Peace Prize with the fortune he made from the invention to promote peace instead of war.

Neutron bomb

Neutron bombs release a mass of subatomic particles called neutrons, but do not produce much of a physical blast.

The burst of neutrons destroys living things – including humans – but leaves buildings and other structures untouched.

The world's first aerial bombardment was in 1849 when Austria attacked Venice – using unmanned hot-air balloons!

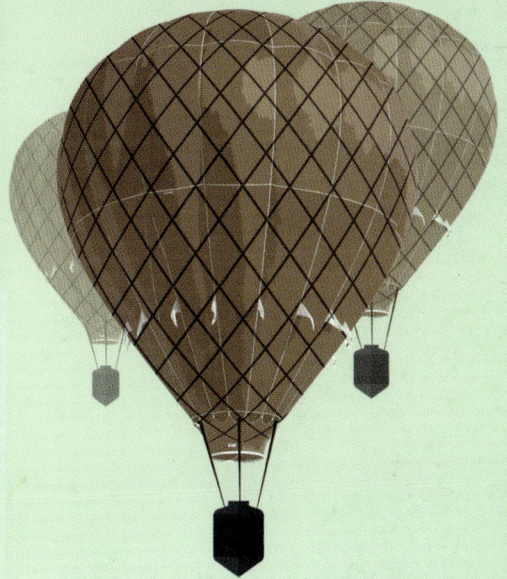

Honey bees, with just a little training, might help detect mines with their super-sensitive sense of smell.

Mines

Mines are hidden bombs that are usually detonated by pressure. Often buried just underground, they make large areas dangerous for many years. Mine-hunting has long relied on metal detectors, but safer methods are in the planning stage. One involves spraying land with a type of bacteria that glows when it is near explosives.

19

Radar

Radio waves, which also provide us with entertainment and news, can be used to sense objects using a technique called radar – 'radio detection and ranging'. A transmitter sends out radio waves and then 'listens' for when they come back and from which direction. Radar became an important tool during the Second World War.

Finding the enemy

Reconnaissance, or information gathering about an enemy, is an essential element in warfare. Over the years, methods have included smoke signals, bonfires burning on hilltops and even sending pigeons off to deliver messages to people behind enemy lines. The twentieth century saw the range of tools widened considerably, thanks to new scientific developments.

Hot-air balloons and powered aircraft entered the world of warfare as reconnaissance tools, allowing armies to observe enemy troops and equipment from above.

Sonar

Sonar, or Sound Navigation and Ranging, uses a similar technique to radar (but with sound rather than radio waves). Sonar equipment sends out sound waves and then measures their echo, once they've bounced off enemy vessels, to find these vessels' exact locations.

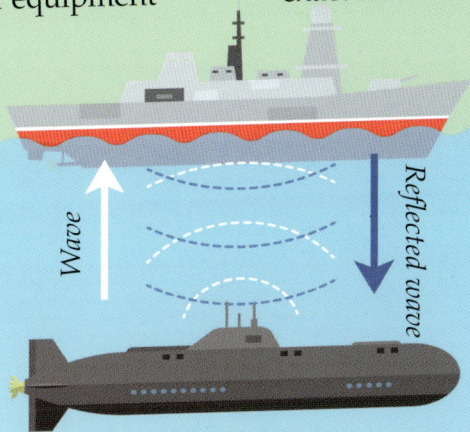

Wave

Reflected wave

Bats use the same technique as radar by sending out high-pitched sounds and then waiting for the echoes to return: the method is called echolocation.

Night vision

Some rifle sights and goggles allow soldiers to see in the dark. The devices detect infrared radiation, a type of light not normally visible to the human eye.

Why it works

The US Navy has a squad of about 80 bottle-nosed dolphins to help with reconnaissance work. The dolphins are trained to detect underwater mines and to drop an electronic device called a transponder when they find one. Naval divers then use sound-detection equipment to find the transponder, so they can destroy the explosives.

During the American War of Independence, the American rebels often wore beige or brown clothing, which blended in with the forest background. The British soldiers, with their bright red uniforms, were far easier to spot and to shoot at.

The unseen enemy

Just as detecting an enemy is important in warfare, trying not to be detected – or not allowing a weapon to be detected – can be crucial. Once again, science provides the way to achieve these aims.

Camouflage

Just as leopards and other animals have colouring or patterns that 'blend in', military clothing and equipment can be designed to resemble the background vegetation or landscape of a battlefield.

Stealth bomber

A new range of aircraft bombers, called stealth bombers, are built or coated with materials that reduce the reflection of radio waves, visible light or other forms of radiation. This lets the planes enter airspace without being detected by radar or other forms of tracking.

Can you believe it?

The American military is developing a technology that can bend light and hide an object (or person) – just like a magic cloak of invisibility.

Poison gas

Not quite unseen (it often had a yellowish-brown tint), poisonous mustard gas would drift silently across First World War battlefields. It killed or seriously injured anyone who wasn't wearing a protective mask.

Scientists believe that being colour-blind might actually be an advantage when looking at camouflage. Colour-blind people rely on differences of light and dark, rather than of slightly different colours, to detect patterns.

Direct hits

Nuclear weapons have only been used twice – their firepower devastated the Japanese cities of Hiroshima and Nagasaki at the end of the Second World War.

Going nuclear

The amazing energy contained in some of the tiniest particles – atoms – has been harnessed to provide electricity, but also to create the world's most destructive weapons. Nuclear weapons depend either on 'splitting' atoms to release energy in a process called fission or slamming atoms together (fusion).

Enrico Fermi, the scientist who first 'split the atom' to usher in the nuclear age in 1942, was confident – but not 100 % sure – that he'd be able to stop the chain reaction before it destroyed the world.

Wolves of the sea

Nuclear-armed submarines patrol the oceans, prepared to launch missiles at a moment's notice. They can navigate dark waters thanks to satellite communication (GPS).

The 'Star Wars' defence plan

Under the abandoned Strategic Defence Initiative (nicknamed 'Star Wars') orbiting US satellites would zap enemy's nuclear missiles.

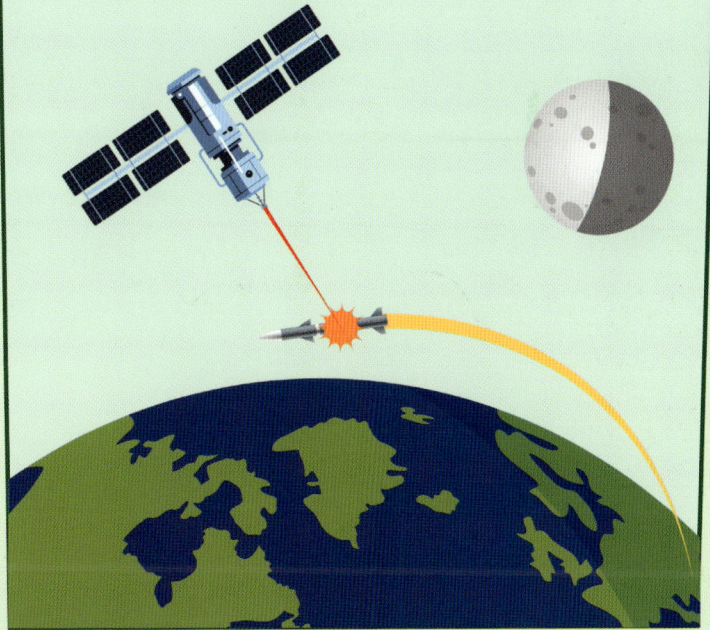

Try it yourself

You can create a 'non-nuclear' chain reaction by lining up a series of books, close to each other but not touching.

Give the end book a tap so that it tips into the next book, which tips into the third book, and so on right down the line.

Hydrogen bombs are 1,000 times more powerful than the atomic bombs dropped on Hiroshima and Nagasaki.

25

Many of the most modern mine-detecting vehicles can be operated without a driver, reducing casualties.

Remote control

The safest weapons are the ones that remain in the battlefield while the operator is out of fire, some distance away. In some cases, the operators might be halfway across the globe; other times, they can see the effects first-hand. Cutting-edge technology fuels these weapons developments.

Robot cannons

Naval vessels equipped with remote-controlled turrets were designed to combat modern piracy, but they can be put to use in combat just as readily.

'Smart bombs'

Precision-guided munition, better known as 'smart bombs', can be guided by radio or lasers to find and destroy a target with great accuracy.

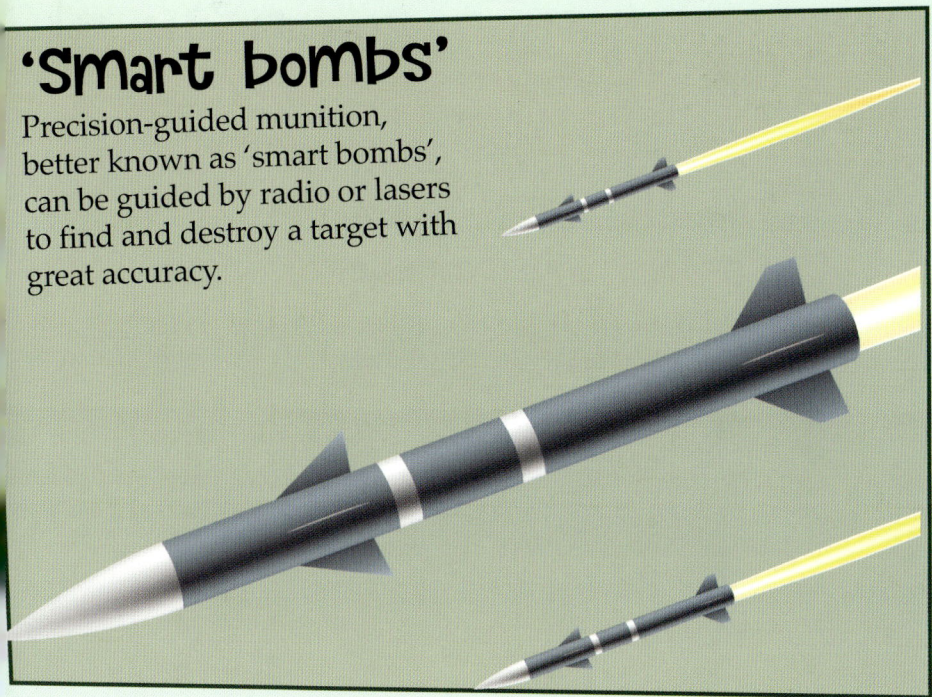

Drones

Drones, mini-helicopters guided remotely, have become common sights around the world. Not surprisingly, drone technology has been used to deliver weapons and messages across battle zones.

The US Navy has a top-secret department devoted to training dolphins and sea lions to detect mines, find missing objects and even help endangered swimmers.

Fascinating fact

Drones that are smaller than a baby's hand could potentially use cameras and facial recognition to hunt down and attack individual humans.

27

Lasers

Super-concentrated beams of light called lasers have already been put to a wide range of uses in industry and medicine. Those same beams can also be powerful weapons, and are likely to be used increasingly in the future.

Looking ahead

Scientific and technological advances in the past have spilled over into the world of warfare and conflict. There's nothing to suggest that the pattern won't continue in the future. Maybe it could save lives by allowing non-humans to fight it out – or could it signal even greater dangers for the human race?

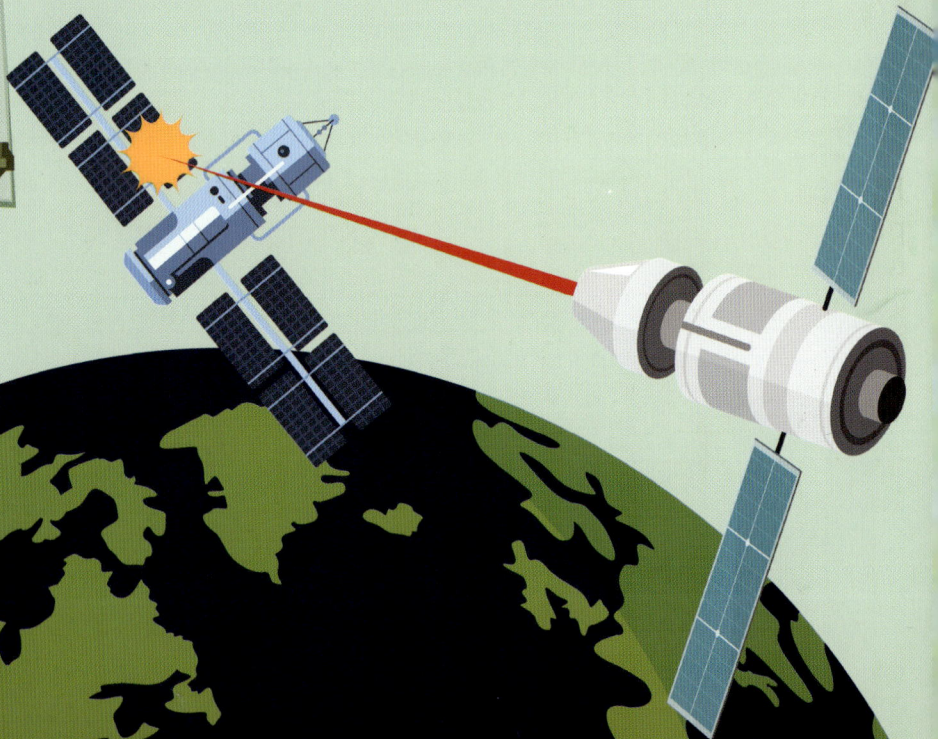

Some scientists believe that spacecraft equipped with powerful nuclear weapons could be used against dangers from outer space, like large asteroids on possible collision courses with our planet.

Cyber weapons

Computer experts have already found ways of 'hacking' (accessing without permission) the important software networks of businesses and even countries. Imagine the power of a cyber weapon that could disable an enemy's entire military system at the touch of a few keys.

Some of the most advanced technology still depends on rare minerals extracted from the earth. In the future, countries where those minerals are present could use their supply as weapons.

Artificial intelligence

For decades, people have predicted that computers in the future could 'think for themselves', without needing humans to instruct them. This form of Artificial Intelligence could become a major feature in future conflicts.

Can you believe it?

The latest weapons might not be so modern, after all. Some records suggest that the Greek scientist Archimedes made an early laser beam. He is said to have built a set of 'burning mirrors' to protect the port of Syracuse by reflecting the Sun's rays and burning an attacking Roman fleet in 212 BC.

Glossary

Artificial Intelligence The ability of computers to make decisions without being given commands from humans.

Atom The smallest unit of a pure substance (like gold or oxygen), forming the basis of all matter in the Universe.

Atomic bomb A powerful weapon that harnesses the energy released from a chain reaction.

Ballistic missile A missile that travels in a steep arch-like path when it is fired.

Ballistics The science that studies the path of bullets, shells and other objects that are fired.

Camouflage The way of covering or colouring something so that it blends in with its surroundings, making it harder to recognise.

Chain reaction A reaction in the nucleus of an atom that releases enough energy to create a series of similar reactions.

Crossbow A weapon that attaches a bow to a wooden support and has a crank to draw the bow back to fire a bolt.

D-Day Landings The largest seaborne invasion in history, when more than 160,000 soldiers landed in France on the 6th of June, 1944.

Detonate Cause to explode or fire.

Energy The power to move something using force.

Facial Recognition A method of identification that records and later recognises human faces.

Fission A nuclear reaction that occurs when an object collides with the nucleus of an atom, causing it to split.

Force The push or pull on an object when it meets another object.

Four-wheel drive An engine system that provides power to the front and rear axles, so that all four wheels are powered.

Fusion A nuclear reaction in which the nuclei of some atoms fuse together to form a heavier nucleus, releasing energy.

GPS An abbreviation of Global Positioning System, a method of locating a position on Earth by communicating with satellites.

Hydrogen bomb A weapon that releases enormous power through nuclear fusion.

Kinetic energy The energy that an object has because of its motion.

Lever A basic tool to lift or pry things.

Medieval Describing the historical period of roughly AD 500 to AD 1500, and sometimes called the Middle Ages.

Neutron A subatomic particle, having no electrical charge, in the nucleus of an atom.

Nucleus (plural nuclei) The positively charged core of an atom, containing positively charged protons and neutrons with no charge at all.

Potential energy Stored energy due to an object's relative position.

Radar A radio device that measures the strength of echoes to determine the position and movement of distant objects.

Shell A cylinder-shaped explosive fired by a cannon.

Siege A military operation in which enemy forces surround and isolate a fortress or settlement.

Software Written codes or programs that operate a computer.

Subatomic particle Any of the particles smaller than an atom.

Transponder A device for receiving a radio signal and immediately transmitting a different signal.

Turbine An engine driven by moving liquid or steam pushing against rotating blades attached to a central shaft.

Index